W9-BYZ-730

CELTIC BLESSINGS

COMPILED BY RAY SIMPSON

CELTIC
BLESSINGS

*

Prayers for
Everyday Life

LOYOLAPRESS.
CHICAGO

LOYOLAPRESS.

3441 N. Ashland Avenue
Chicago, Illinois 60657

First North American edition 1999
© 1998 by Ray Simpson. All rights reserved.

Published in Great Britain by Hodder and Stoughton Ltd.

Scripture quotations marked *NRSV* are from the New Revised Standard Version Bible: Catholic Edition copyright © 1993 and 1989 by the Division of Christian Education of the National Council of the Churches of Christ in the U.S.A. Used by permission. All rights reserved. Those marked *NIV* are from the Holy Bible, New International Version copyright © 1973, 1978, 1984 by the International Bible Society. Used by permission of Zondervan Publishing House. Those marked *NEB* are from the New English Bible copyright © 1961, 1970 by the Delegates of the Oxford University Press and the Syndics of the Cambridge University Press. Those marked *TEV* are from the Good News Bible, Today's English Version copyright © 1983 by Thomas Nelson, Inc.

Interior design by Jeanne Calabrese Design

Library of Congress Cataloging-in-Publication Data
Celtic blessings: prayers for everyday life/compiled by Ray Simpson.

p. cm.
ISBN 0-8294-1344-8
1. Prayers. 2. Benediction. 3. Celtic Church — Prayer-books and devotions — English. I. Simpson, Ray.
BV245.C396 1999
242'.8 — dc21   98-36977
                                                                 CIP

Printed in Canada
01 02 03 04 05 Webcom 10 9 8 7 6 5 4 3 2

Contents

Introduction

Our society believes in the greatest choice for the greatest number of people. So why should we limit blessings to a few formal occasions in church? God likes everyone! It is time to put some meaning back into that time-honored phrase "and every blessed thing." Why shouldn't everything be blessed? Our forebears, the Celts, had blessings for just about everything, from getting dressed to milking the cow. Home life, work life, travel, birth, death, and everything in between got blessed.

The Christian Bible scholar Claus Westermann reminds us that God deals with his people in two main ways[1] by delivering them from what is bad and by blessing what is good in their lives: "So the LORD brought us out of Egypt with a mighty hand and an outstretched arm. . . . He brought us to this place and gave us this land, a land flowing with milk and honey" (Deuteronomy 26:8 – 9, *NIV*). In the Old Testament, blessing included both the spiritual and the material aspects of life. Another scholar reminds us that "blessing is life, health, and fertility for the people, their cattle, their fields . . . blessing is the basic power of life itself."[2] Abraham, whom Christians, Jews, and Muslims call their spiritual father, has his entire vocation carved out for him in terms of blessing. He is told by God:

> "Go from your country and your kindred and your father's house to the land that I will show you. I will make of you a great nation, and I will bless you, and make your name great, so that you will be a blessing. I will bless those who bless you, and the one who curses you I will curse; and in you all the families of the earth shall be blessed."
>
> So Abram went, as the LORD had told him. (Genesis 12:1 – 4, *NRSV*)

When Jacob gave his final blessings to the twelve clans that had begun to grow out of his twelve sons, he gave each son a blessing that was appropriate to his character and circumstances (Genesis 49). Blessings of a whole tribe were passed on through a father to his sons.

We can learn two important lessons from this. First, a blessing is mediated along the lines of relationship. Once relationships are severed, the blessing is dissipated. To go around blessing people or objects in a perfunctory way is magic; it is not of God. Second, the work of blessing is most effective when it is linked with knowledge, wisdom, or the gift of "seeing" that Jacob possessed.

Christ demonstrated the dual work of deliverance and blessing, and he asked his apostles to continue a work of "binding and loosing" (i.e., blessing) people (Matthew 16:19). Christ's final act before his ascension was to bless his assembled apostles (Luke 24:50 – 51). This action gave them a visible sign of his earlier promise: "I am with you always, to the end of the age" (Matthew 28:20, NRSV). It served as a model for the blessing that is bestowed by pastors, parents, friends, and others in the name of Christ. Through the hands of the apostles and their successors, the Lord continues to bless his people even now.

Why, then, have we lost sight of the importance of blessing in all aspects of life? Since Augustine, the influential fourth-century theologian, there has been a tendency in Western Christianity to emphasize the evil in human life from which we need deliverance, but to fail to emphasize the good in human life and in creation that we need to bless. This is like looking at the world through spectacles that have only one lens. If one looks at the world to see what is wrong with it without also looking to see what is right with it, a jaundiced outlook sets in. By using spectacles with the lens of sin but without the lens of goodness, we have lost sight of the theology and the practice of blessing. Yet they are an essential part of our biblical birthright that we need to recover.

Fortunately, the Celtic church never forgot the value of blessing, and the resurgence of Celtic Christianity helps to restore blessing to us. The Celtic church understands that it is Christ who gives the blessing. An Eastern Orthodox priest shares this understanding when he bestows a blessing: his fingers are arranged to form the letters *ICXC*, an abbreviation in Greek letters for "Jesus Christ." This signifies that the blessing is Christ's, not that of a mere human.

The pre-Christian Celts used to call down blessings from the sun on all sorts of everyday things. As they said a blessing, they made a circle with their hands in the direction of the sun as it moved from its rising in the east to its setting in the west. The Christians took this as a good instinct but gave their blessings in the name of the Triune God, who created the sun. They called the making of a circle the *Caim*, which they did three times, once each in the name of the Father, the Son, and the Spirit, often referred to as The Three. In this way, everything under the sun was blessed, encircled, and protected.

Brigid of Ireland was a great blesser and a potent symbol of blessing. Through her, God mediated compassion, energy, fertility, and healing. She often helped her mother, who, though a Christian, was a hard-working slave of a druid priest. A song Brigid sang as she churned the butter begins "Mary's Son, my friend, come to bless this kitchen. May we have fullness through you." Through Brigid, the Lord multiplied the butter as once he multiplied the loaves and fishes. The following prayer from the *Carmina Gadelica*[3] always brings to mind Brigid in her kitchen:

> You who put beam in moon and sun,
> You who put food in ear and herd,
> You who put fish in stream and sea,
> Send the butter up to me.
> Come, you rich lumps, come!
> Come, you rich lumps, come!
> Come, you rich lumps, masses large,
> Come, you rich lumps, come!

At Columba's monastery on Iona, every person on the island — and the animals — walked sunwise around the Angels Hill on Michaelmas Day to bring a blessing on the island for the coming year. Columba blessed all sorts of things with the sign of the cross: the milking pail, the work tools, the pen that the writing might be to the glory of God, the seed that the crops might be saved from harm.

The blessings and prayers of the Western Highlanders of Scotland, collected in the nineteenth century by Alexander Carmichael in the *Carmina Gadelica*, carry on this tradition. Nothing is too earthly or too small to be included in a blessing. Not only is each cow included but each teat as well! The *Carmina Gadelica* recounts the story of a poor old woman whose husband had died and whose son had drowned. She was left with three orphans to care for, but her heifer would produce neither milk nor calf. She sought Columba's help. Columba made up a song of blessing that he sang to her heifer with tears streaming down his cheeks, and then he taught her to sing it, too:

> My heifer, beloved, be not alone
> Let your little calf be before you.
>
> Coax your pretty one to yourself
> Till you send to the fold a herd.

> Certain is the gentle proverb
> The cow of blessings is the cow of calves.
>
> The black heifer is reconciled
> You will be lowing to your pretty one.
>
> You will come home with droves
> You will quench the thirst of hundreds.

The poor woman crooned this blessing to her heifer, and the cow took her calf. This is an example of a prophetic blessing, like the blessings of Jacob in the Bible. The prayer of faith calls forth what is being blessed in words so that it becomes a reality.

Catherine Maclennon, one of the Highlanders who passed on to Alexander Carmichael the words of blessings that had become part of the fabric of their lives, once told him:

> My mother would be asking us to sing our morning song to God down in the back-house, as Mary's lark was singing it up in the clouds and as Christ's mavis was singing it yonder in the tree, giving glory to the God of the creatures for the repose of night, for the light of day, and for the joy of life. She would tell us that every creature on the earth here below and in the ocean beneath and in the air above was giving glory to the great God of the creatures and the worlds, of the virtues and the blessings, and would *we* be dumb!

How to Use This Book

There are blessings in this book for every aspect of our lives today. The first section contains specific blessings for everyday events. See the contents list to find one that is appropriate as you need it.

The second section responds to requests for Celtic touches to formal occasions such as infant blessings, baptisms, house blessings, and weddings. Some of these are in the form of services; others are to complement the normal services. It is best to read the services through first and choose the sections that you wish to use before you make the arrangements with family, friends, and any clergy. You will need to decide beforehand whether to invite a priest, another minister, or a soul friend (i.e., a friend who has a spiritual rapport with what you will pledge in the service) to help lead the service. Where a space is left blank, the name of the person for whom blessing is sought (or the parent, sibling, etc.) should be inserted.

The third section is for routine use and contains blessings for different times of each day and for different seasons of each year. The final section has blessings for personal use at significant stages in one's journey through life.

Throughout the book, you can apply a blessing to yourself rather than to others by interchanging "you" for "me," etc.

> *Ray Simpson*
> *Lindisfarne Retreat*
> *Holy Island*

NOTES

[1]Claus Westermann, *Blessing in the Bible and the Life of the Church* (Philadelphia, 1978), 1 – 15, quoted in Matthew Fox, *Original Blessing* (Bear & Co., 1983).

[2]Sigmund Mowinckel, trans. D.R. Ap-Thomas, *The Psalms in Israel's Worship*, vol. 2 (Blackwell, 1967), 44.

[3]Alexander Carmichael, ed., *Carmina Gadelica* (Floris Books, 1992), 341.

1

Everyday Blessings

Family and Friends

Fathers

God help you to
listen to your loved ones
play with your loved ones
laugh with your loved ones
weep with your loved ones
forgive your loved ones
take responsibility for your loved ones
be faithful to your loved ones
forever.

Bless you fathers,
May you be priests
to your wives and children.

Mother

Mother, dear,
pearl of great price,
too often have we taken you for granted.

May the Holy Trinity protect you
May the Three of limitless love renew you

so that

An island shall you be in our seas
A light shall you be in our nights
A well shall you be in our deserts
until heaven's arms enfold you, too.

Grandparent

May this little one bring
Love and affection to you
And good to the earth.

May this be a day of grace for you.

May you be a guarding one to this gift of heaven
Along with the saints and the angels
and the Three of limitless love.

Toddler

This blessing should be said when washing the toddler.

The three palmfuls of the Sacred Three
To preserve you from every envy or evil eye:
The palmful of the Father of life;
The palmful of the Christ of love;
The palmful of the Spirit of peace,
The God of threefold love.

Stepchildren

The family of God to draw round you
The family of God to welcome you
The family of God to listen to you
The family of God to cherish you
The family of God to heal you
Mary the mother of our Lord
Joseph at his work
All the saints of heaven
Your guardian angels
And we your new loved ones.

May heaven's gates of welcome open wide
May our heart of welcome open wide
May your heart of welcome open wide
This day and always.

Friends

Beauty of friendship grow between us
Friendship
without guile
without malice
without striving.

Goodness of friendship grow between us
Friendship
with light
with wings
with soul sharing.

Be in the eye of each friend
of my journey
to bless and to teach each one.

The eye of the Father be upon us
The eye of the Son be upon us
The eye of the Spirit be upon us
The eye of the Friendly Three
be upon us forever.

House Blessings

At the Entrance

May this house be built upon the Rock of rocks, the rock of Christ; so that no onslaught can undermine it, and no ill wind can unsettle it. May the guardian angel welcome all who enter this place, and repel all who would harm it.

Blessed water may be sprinkled on the door and used to make the sign of the cross upon it with a finger. (This may be repeated in each room.) Inside, the sign of the cross is made or a cross is hung in the hall with the following words:

We invite you, O Christ, to be the master of this household and of everything in it. May the cross of Christ be between you and all that has happened here in the past.

In the Kitchen

We consecrate this kitchen to you. May the
deep peace of the Son of Mary possess all
who work amidst the clatter of this place; may
all be done in a spirit of humble service, may
all be done as for you. Bless the washing, bring
forth fullness in the cooking, put your glory
in the working.

In the Living Room

We place into your hands all those who will live
together here. May they know that everything
here is yours and that they belong here. May
they sense your love here. May the presence of
the Three Kindly Persons free each to accept
their pain, to grow through each stage of their
development, to give space to each other, to
express their feelings, to forgive from their hearts,
to flower as persons.

In the Dining Room

Bless this room. May the eating be a celebration of God's goodness. May the feasting be a fellowship with God's friends. As you drink the sweet fruits of creation, may you drink the sweetness of God's life, and be preserved from the poisons of envy.

This prayer is sometimes attributed to St. Brigid and may be read by a new resident:

I would prepare a feast and be host to the great High King, with all the company of heaven.

The sustenance of pure love be in my house, the roots of repentance in my house. Baskets of love be mine to give, with cups of mercy for all the company. Sweet Jesus, be there with us, with all the company of heaven. May cheerfulness abound in the feast, the feast of the great High King, my host for all eternity.

In Each Bedroom

In the name of the eternal Father, in the name of the loving Son, in the name of the gentle Spirit, the friendly Three-in-One: bless and make holy this room, and may angels guard all who sleep here. That part of you that did not grow at morning, may it grow at night. That part of you that did not grow at night, may it grow in the morning.

In a Couple's Bedroom

This blessing may be said in addition to the one above.

God give you delight and tenderness in your
    lying together.
God give you peace and forgiveness in your
    sleeping together.
God give you solitude and freedom to be
    yourselves for each other.

In a Child's Room

May the loving Father God always be here with you and make you feel safe. May friendly Jesus always be here with you and make you feel happy. May the kindly Spirit always be here with you to listen to you. May you enjoy their company as you play. May angels look after you when you sleep, and when you dream, and may they help you to wake with a smile on your face.

In a Guest Room

This blessing may be said in addition to the words for each bedroom.

Fill this room with a spirit of hospitality. May each person who sleeps here be enfolded in the loving arms of the Savior.

In a Workroom or Playroom

Bless the work, the play, or the study done
here. Make fruitful the reading, the writing,
the planning. May all that is done reflect
the peace and order of creation.

Bathrooms

May all who bathe their bodies here bathe them
in the mild rays of the Sun of suns, as Mary
bathed Christ in the rich milk of Egypt. The
sweetness of Christ be in your mouth as you
clean your teeth; the beauty of Christ be upon
your face as you comb your hair; the love of
Christ flow over you as you wash your frame.

As you look in the mirror may you see
The hands of Mary washing you,
The hands of angels cleansing you,
The hands of the saints straightening you,
The hands of Jesus restoring you.

For Pets and Other Creatures

Dear Lord, may all that is here reflect the
harmony and wholeness that you want for
all creation.

May the cat(s) purr with the pleasure
of friendship;
May the dog(s) wag tail(s) with the delight
of meetings;
May [*name the pet*] be happy and healthy;
May the wild creatures find nature here
is friendly;
May the birds find food here and chirp
with gladness.

In the Garden

If there is a party, barbecue, or social gathering, this Caim *prayer is said by all, if appropriate, after walking in a circle round the property:*

All:

Circle this place by day and by night;
Circle it in winter, circle it in summer.
Look down upon it with your smile;
Lift it up with your strength.
Keep far from it all that harms;
Keep all that's good within Christ's arms.

May this place be fragrant with the presence of
the Lord;
May this place overflow with the gratitude of
his people;
May this place echo with the sounds of joy;
May clouds of God's peace envelop it;
God's peace be always here and in those who
dwell here.
Let us enjoy his presence now.

All:

Amen.

Discerning of Spirits

This may be done in homes upon request. After a silent waiting on God, name any spirit or influence that is felt to be present and not of God, e.g., a clinical, a restless, an angry, a fearful, an unclean, or an evil spirit. Water may be sprinkled or a short house Communion performed, showing forth the dying, rising, and victory of Christ over all powers, past and present, seen and unseen. Passages from the Bible such as Philippians 2:1–11 may be read, together with the following:

Almighty Father, victorious Savior, Holy Spirit, you are stronger than the elements, stronger than the shadows, stronger than the fears, stronger than human wills, stronger than the spirits; we enthrone you in this place and lift you up with our praise.

A hymn may be sung.

In the name of the crucified and risen Christ, we set this place free from the power of the past. In the name of Christ we say to all powers that do not reverence him as Lord: be gone from this place. Be gone.

Home

Don't take worries about those left behind; release them.
These prayers can help in doing this.

When Away from Home

We release into your hands, O Lord,
     our homes
Those whom we love and care for
Any who are dependent on us who may
     feel vulnerable without us.
Lord, you love those whom we love.

We release into your hands, O Lord,
Those for whom we have responsibilities
Those who are in need at this time
Those we have supported
Lord, you care for all those for whom
     we care.

We release into your hands, O Lord, our work
The pressures that weary us
The problems that would pursue us
The things we have forgotten
The tasks left unfinished.
Lord, you rule over all things.

Arriving in a New Place

Lord, we offer you our conflicting feelings
Our apprehensions and our aspirations,
The strange bed, the changed roles, the fear of
     the unknown.

Risen Christ, we acknowledge that you are in
     our midst,
Circle this place and make it your own
Keep peace within, keep evil out.
May all memories, influences, or powers that
     are not of you flee from this place
May the angels guard and welcome us.

We turn our eyes upon you,
Calm us and settle us
Help us to feel at home with you and with
    one another
So there is no need to pretend.
Help us to be ourselves
And to see these new faces as our family.

On Returning Home

God of the fray, God of the bumps
Cool me down, because I am frayed.
Lift me up, because I have come down with
    a bump.
Help me to accept the duties that confront me.
Help me to assimilate the experiences that have
    enriched me
And to become aware of your presence
Now in the present moment.

School

Going to School

May smiling faces welcome you
May helping hands welcome you
May kind teachers welcome you

May
fears fly away
temper go away
lies stay away.

May you
make new friends
learn new things
grow strong limbs.

May
God make you thoughtful
Jesus make you happy
Spirit make you friendly.

At School

Lord, circle this school
and keep these good things within:

eagerness to learn
flowering of talents
a sense of wonder
enjoyment of sport
experience of beauty
warmth of friendship
the art of listening
respect for all
service of others
teamwork between children and adults
care for the planet
reverence for life
fitness of body, mind and spirit.

Lord, circle this school
and keep these bad things without:

low self-esteem
confusion
prejudice
pride
bullying
cheating
stealing
fear of appraisal
malicious gossip
absenteeism
"couldn't care less" attitudes.

Lord, circle this school
for you are the source of all that is good
    and true.
Amen.

Exams

Every subject, whether it be art or language, home economics or computer technology, reflects something of the nature of God. As we name and bless a forthcoming exam, we relax, and this helps to bring out the best in us.

I bless this exam
in the name of the Designer of truth.
I bless this exam
in the name of the Protector from ill.
I bless this exam
in the name of the Spirit who guides.
Open my eyes to see how this subject
reflects something of you.
Aid me to understand this subject
with my heart as well as with my head.
Give me
Wisdom to know the nub of things,
Strength to recall what is useful,
Peace to leave the result to you.

Graduation

Dear God
I've come to the end of my school years
with mixed feelings.
As I look back
And as I look to what is coming,
I see all sorts of shapes and colors
In flow and flux.
God of shapes and colors
Bless these to me
And be in the flow and flux.

As I look back
And as I look to what is coming,
I see all sorts of empty gaps
In flux and flow.
God of the gaps
Fill these for me
And be in the flux and flow.

As I look back
Bless me with forgiveness
And the knowledge that
Nothing need be wasted with you.

As I look forward
How can I find out what work is right for me?
Bless my questioning and finding out.
Will I get a job?
Bless me to my work
All the talents you have put within me
May they grow wherever I shall be.

Be a vision to guide me
A voice to lead me
A Savior to forgive me
A hand to hold me
A friend to teach me
Always.

Work and Career

Work Blessing

May my work be faithful
May my work be honest
May my work be blessed
May my work bless others
May my work bless you.

May the wealth and work of the world
be available to all
and for the exploitation of none.

May managers, employees, and shareholders work
together like fingers on a hand.

Computers

I program my computer
with the love of God.
God be with me now
as I call words into being.
May they make real my work of love.
May they join the work of creation.
Called from nothing, uttered over chaos
bringing order.

Esther de Waal

Joining Up

It is a mistake to reserve prayers only for the "nice" aspects of life. Some people are called to serve in the armed services, in emergency services, or in a political or campaigning movement that is far from cozy.

The first three requests in the following blessing come from the motto of Ireland's Fianna.

May you have
truth in your hearts
strength in your hands
consistency in your tongues
and love in your being.

New Task

When we begin some new task, whether it is voluntary or paid, it is good to make a rededication of ourselves to God, with others.

Speaker:

In blessing our foreheads

All:

we reclaim the powers of reason

Speaker:

In blessing our eyes

All:

we reclaim the power of vision

Speaker:

In blessing our lips

All:

we reclaim the power to speak

Speaker:

In blessing our hands

All:

we reclaim the power of creativity

Speaker:

In blessing our feet

All:

we reclaim the power of movement

Money

Many of us receive money weekly or monthly, either directly or paid into an account. Sometimes we receive an extra or unexpected sum of money. We call such money a "windfall." This windfall can be either a blessing or a curse, so it is important to bring it to God from the first.

Good be on you, gift from heaven
Wisdom be on you, gift from heaven
Restraint be on you, gift from heaven
Thought be on you, gift from heaven
The Giver be on you, gift from heaven
Jesus be on you, gift from heaven
The Spirit be on you, gift from heaven

Now that you have begun the practice of blessing special amounts of money, why not practice this blessing of money whenever you receive your regular income?

Achievements

New Job

Bless to me, O God, everything my eye
   shall see
Bless to me, O God, everything my hand
   shall do
Bless to me, O God, everything my brain
   shall think
Bless to me, O God, the place and
   the equipment.
Bless to me, O God, the people we shall
   serve through our work.

Be in the interruptions and the setbacks
Be in the eye of the person who is difficult
Be in the eye of the person who is a delight.

Promotion

⁀&

A proportion of us are promoted or invited to accept some office of greater responsibility at one time or another. This may be in national or local government, education, business, media, church, or elsewhere. This, too, should be marked before God and before one's family.

This blessing reflects advice from Cormac, who was known as the Irish Solomon, to those who were to become kings or warriors. Cormac observed that it was through these habits that the young could become kingly.

God's blessing be upon you for this new office.
May you be
Not too conceited or you will lose the bonds
    of trust
Not too naive or you will be deceived
Not too diffident or you will fail to convince
Not too talkative or you will not be heard
Not too silent or you will not be heeded
Not too hard or you will be broken
Not too feeble or you will be disregarded.

Sports

This is a suitable prayer to say on return home after someone has completed a marathon, won a medal, or been part of a team that has competed in a contest.

We bless you, God, for the goodness of this
    achievement.

The strength of the ox be yours
The speed of a gazelle be yours
The suppleness of fish be yours
The flight of a bird be yours
The joy of the earth be yours
The warmth of the sun be yours.

The wreath of God around your neck
The wreath of God around your chest
The wreath of God around your thighs
The wreath of God around your feet

And the gold everlasting.

Illness and Injury

*Jesus sometimes spoke in a direct, pithy way to disease: "be
clean" (of leprosy), Matthew 8:8; "come out" (of a demon),
Luke 4:35; "wash" (to cure blindness), John 9:7. These prayers,
mostly from the* Carmina Gadelica, *direct God's power to a
particular part of the anatomy.*

Talking to the Diseased Organ

To [*name of affected organ*]:
The God of gods
The Healer of healers,
The Spirit of eternity,
The perfect Three of power
Restore you.

To a Stye

Go back! go back! go back!
You thievish rascal of the stye!

For the Removal of a Microbe in the Body

May God search for them, may God remove them
From your blood, from your flesh, from
    your urine,
From your smooth fragrant bones;
From your close veins, from your hard kidney,
From your pith, from your marrow, dear one,
From this day and every day
Till the day you shall end your life.

To a Blind or Affected Eye While Bathing or Touching It

Pour, King of life,
Pour, Christ of peace,
Pour, Spirit of cleansing.

You who created the orb
And placed the pupil in the eye,
Search the mystery within the lid,
Befriend its sight, O God.
Make whole this day the eye;
Restore this day the sight.

When Laying Hands on a Painful Part of the Body

Power of heaven have I over you;
Power of universe have I over you;
Power of sun have I over you;
Power of earth have I over you;
Power of God have I over you.
Powers of God, work God's will in you.

For Any Disease of the Body

May the strong Lord of life
Destroy your disease of body
From the crown of your head
To the base of your heel.
With the power of the Christ of love
And the Creator of the seasons,
With the aid of the Holy Spirit,
And the powers of wholeness together.

For a Swelling

Peace come into this swelling,
The peace of the King of power.
Subsiding come to your swelling.

Look, O Christ, on this swelling,
Since you are the King of power
Give rest to this person.
Bring the microbe out of this tumor.
Be whole. Let your swelling now shrink.
In the holy presence of the Father,
In the holy presence of the Son,
In the holy presence of the Spirit,
The holy presence of compassion.

For Any Skin or Blood Disease

May God heal you, my dear one.
I am now placing my hand on you
In the name of Father, Son, and Spirit of virtue,
Three Persons who encompass you forever.
Full healing come to your blood,
Perfect healing to your soft flesh,
Another healing to your smooth skin,
In the name of the powers of the Holy Three.

Miscarriage

Bible Readings

Some people brought children to Jesus for him
to place his hands on them, but the disciples
scolded the people. When Jesus noticed this,
he was angry and said to his disciples, "Let the
children come to me, and do not stop them,
because the kingdom of God belongs to such
as these." (Mark 10:13 – 14, *TEV*)

[Jesus said:] "See that you don't despise any of
these little ones. Their angels in heaven, I tell
you, are always in the presence of my good
Father in heaven." (Matthew 18:10, *TEV*)

A Parent's Prayer

Dear Lord Jesus, kind and loving Friend, you
were always glad to be in the company
of children; you taught us that we must be
like them in the kingdom of heaven. I now
realize that I have more children than at
first it seemed.

The child who was lost through miscarriage is
mine and yours.

I give this child the name [*name of child*]

I pray that you will heal the scars of [*name
of child*]

May [*name of child*] be enfolded in your love.

May s/he find healing.

Set [*name of child*] free from all shock of hurt
that hinders their journey into wholeness in
your kingdom, so that [*name of child*] may
live with you in light and joy forever. I look
forward to that day when, through faith in
Jesus Christ, we may be reunited in paradise.

**A Friend's Prayer
for the Deceased Child**

We release [*name of child*] into your hands. May
your blessing and your peace be upon [*name
of child*]. Bring him/her to wholeness in your
eternal kingdom.

When a Person Suffers from Insecurity or a Lack of Identity

An eye was seeing you,
A mouth has named you,
A heart has thought of you,
A mind has desired you.

For a Removal of a Disease of the Spirit

As Christ removed the sleep from the little child
   of the grave,
May he remove from you, dear one,
Each frown, each envy, each malice.

The Healing Rhythm of the Trinity

Common Celtic practice is to perform a healing action three times; this reflects the healing rhythm of the Trinity.

I commend you, [*name of sick person*]
In the eye of God,
In the love of Jesus,
In the name of Spirit,
In Trinity of power.

May Three Persons sanctify you,
May Three Persons help you,
The Father and the Son
And the perfect Spirit.

Healing with Water

*Water is placed in a bowl, and a leaf or sponge is dipped in it
and placed on the affected part with words such as these:*

May this water be for your healing
In the holy name of the Father,
In the holy name of the Son,
In the holy name of the Spirit,
In the holy name of the Three,
Everlasting, kindly, wise.

Injury

I am appealing to you, since you are the King
   of heaven
I am praying to you, since you are the King
   of good
Lift each wasting, each weariness and sickness.

Lift each soreness and discomfort
I am keenly praying to you
Lift each stiffness
As you separate earth from ocean.

Travel

Car

Bless this car to me, O Lord.
Bless me to my car.
Be in my driving
Be in my concentration
Be in my decisions.

Bless this journey to me, O Lord.
It is a small reflection of my journey
    through life,
My way chosen by you.
A journey with you
A journey to you.
A journey to knowing myself
A journey to knowing you
A journey of being saved and healed.

Bless the people I drive by, O Lord.
May they be aware of you in this place.
Bless the owners of the businesses,
May they deal justly and honestly.
Bless the schools, polytechnics, and universities.
Give a teachable spirit to both pupil and teacher.

Carole Parker

New Bicycle

Good speed to you
Good balance to you
Good movement to you.

Power of air to you
Power of wheel to you
Power of frame to you.

Grace of a grateful heart to you
In the name of God
of the starting out
and of the good returning.

New Car

May it bless the earth it will travel on
May it bless the earth that fuels it
May it bless each one who enters it
May it bless each one it passes.

May it be used wisely
May it rest until it is needed
May it be a humble gift to the world
May it be a sign of our good God.
May it go well and be well
Each day and each night of its time.

New Car Owner

May this be a gift of space to you
May this be a gift of movement to you
May this be a gift of sight to you
May this be a gift of meeting to you
In the name of the God
who makes and moves all things.

New Motorcycle

God bless your steed
God bless your speed
Christ meet your need.

By the Spirit be led
And angels overhead
Until you reach your bed.

The Path

God bless the path on which you go
God bless the earth beneath your feet
God bless your destination.

God be a smooth way before you
A guiding star above you
A keen eye behind you
This day, this night, and forever.

God be with you whatever you pass
Jesus be with you whatever you climb
Spirit be with you wherever you stay.

God be with you at each stop and each sea
At each lying down and each rising up
In the trough of the waves, on the crest of
    the billows
Each step of the journey you take.

2
Formal Occasions

*In this section some preparation is needed. The Catholic
church and many Protestant churches have specific liturgies
for sacramental occasions. If these prayers do not fit your
church's liturgy, you may wish to use them with your family
and friends before or after the service.*

Baptism

At the Baptism of an Infant

*When family and friends have gathered, someone may sing a
song, and a priest or another minister may explain the meaning
of baptism.*

**The Signing of the Forehead with the Sign of
the Cross**

The priest, another minister, or a parent says:

I mark you with the sign of the cross

**The person makes the sign of the cross on the
baby's forehead.**

In Brittany, at the cathedral of the Celtic saint Samson of Dol, I saw each member of the baby's family and the godparents in turn make the sign of the cross on the baby's forehead.

Everyone says words such as the following:

May the cross of Christ always be between you
and the evil powers;

May the cross of Christ always be between you
and all ill-will and mishap;

May the cross of Christ always be between you
and everything dark or shameful;

May the cross of Christ always be between you
and all that hurts or harms your soul.

God's Words

As at St. Samson's Cathedral, it is good if the family can take an active part. An older brother, sister, or relative may now read from the Bible.

God's Calling to Parents

Parents may offer encouragement by way of stories or testimonies about how they make the baptism vows real for their children. A mother may tell of how she prays with her infant; a father may say how he prays with and listens to his child.

Blessing the Baby's Future

A person may give a flower, plant, or anything beautiful and natural and say to the parents:

Today we ask that you will try to make your home beautiful so that your child may grow up to appreciate God's beauty.

And to the child:

So today we give you, [*name of child*], this beautiful flower and pray that the personality God has given you will flower into its full beauty.

A person may give a crafted object and say to the parents:

Today we ask that you will try to make your home reflect something of the Creator, by expressing the creativity God has given you and others.

And to the child:

So today we give you, [*name of child*], this crafted present and pray that the creativity God has given you may be fully used.

A person may give to the parents a Bible or book of prayers and say:

Today we ask that you will try in your home to learn about Jesus and to listen to God's voice in the Bible and in your hearts.

And to the child:

So we give you, [*name of child*], this Bible [book] and pray that you will find and follow your calling.

A person may give to a parent, on behalf of the baby, a white candle, saying:

Today we ask that you will make your home a place of faith which radiates the light of Christ.

And to the child:

So we give you, [*name of child*], this candle and pray that you may shine as a light in the world.

All:

Christ as a light illumine and guide you
Christ as a shield overshadow you
Christ under you
Christ over you
Christ beside you on your left and your right
This day be within and without you
Lonely and meek yet all powerful
Be in the mouth of each to whom you
    shall speak
In the mouth of each who shall speak to you
Christ as a light illumine and guide you.

   St. Patrick's Breastplate, adapted

The prayer for birth, "A little drop of your Creator" (page 119), may be said.

At the Baptism of an Older Child or an Adult

This prayer may be said immediately before or after a baptism. If it does not fit into the liturgy, say it when you gather afterwards to celebrate with your friends and family.

Into the life of the Father I immerse you
That he may protect you from harm
Bring you peace and calm.
Into the boundless life of your Maker
    I immerse you.

Into the life of the Son I immerse you
That he may save you from hell
Keep you washed and well.
Into the sinless life of your Savior I immerse you.

Into the life of the Spirit I immerse you
That the Spirit may light up your night
And give you power to do right.
Into the endless life of your Soul Friend
    I immerse you.

Into the life of the Three I immerse you
That they may fill you with love
Lift you to heaven above.
Into the selfless love of the Trinity I immerse you.

Funeral

A blessing is especially meaningful to those who are mourning a loved one. Here are several that can be used before, during, or after the funeral.

Before the Funeral

∿

The Irish wake, at which friends and family gather together around the coffin for food, music, and recounting memories, retains the Celtic idea of celebrating a life. It can be a healing experience to keep the dead person's body in a place where people can see it, sit by it, and put flowers or mementos on it. Some will wish to be silent; others may wish to say a blessing such as this:

Go to your eternal home of welcome
　　my loved companion.
Go into the sleep of Jesus
The restoring sleep of Jesus
The young sleep of Jesus.

Go into the kiss and the peace and the glory
    of Jesus
Into the arms of the Jesus of blessings
Into the generous Christ with his hands
    around you.
Drawing near to the Trinity
Freed from your pains
Pardoned from your sins
Christ beside you bringing peace to your mind.

At the Graveside

*If the deceased person had been baptized, you may ask for water
to be sprinkled over the coffin before the cremation or burial,
and you may ask for words such as these to be spoken:*

May you who were baptized [*state the deceased
    person's baptismal names*]
now be immersed into the life of God:
Into the presence of the Creator I immerse you
Into the presence of the Savior I immerse you
Into the presence of the Spirit I immerse you.

Prayers such as these may be said:

May kindly Michael, chief of the holy angels,
Take charge of your beloved soul
And tenderly bring it home
To the Three of limitless love:
Creator, Savior, Eternal life-giver.

Father, I place [*name of deceased*] into
    your hands;
Acknowledge a sheep of your own fold,
A lamb of your own flock,
A sinner of your own redeeming.
Enfold [*name of deceased*] in the arms of
    your mercy,
In the blessed rest of everlasting peace,
And in the glorious company of the saints
    in light.

    Traditional

Go forth upon your journey from this world,
In the Name of God the Father who created you;
In the Name of Jesus Christ who died for you;
In the Name of the Holy Spirit who shines
    through you;
In friendship with God's saints;
Aided by the holy angels.
May you rest this day in
the peace and love of your eternal home.

Traditional, adapted

May you be as free as the wind
As soft as sheep's wool
As straight as an arrow
That you may journey into the heart of God.

After the Funeral

∾

Grieving, like life itself, is a process. At the funeral we say good-bye, but afterwards we often get more fully in touch with feelings, regrets, longings, memories. The following prayer can be used at an official memorial service, or we can make our own less formal memorial services at any time by finding a quiet space, lighting a candle, looking at a photograph, and slowly, with long pauses, repeating the following prayer:

Holy God, holy and mighty
You alone are Creator
You alone are Savior
You alone are immortal.
We are mortal
formed from the earth
returning to the earth
for you ordained
that we should come from dust and go to dust.
Yet through Christ you ordained also
that with our tears at the dark night of parting
should be mingled the Alleluias

of the glory that pierces the gloom from beyond.
So as we remember the shadows
and as we linger with our precious memories
May we feel your presence
May we be touched by your hope
May we be changed by your glory.

Holy Communion

You can quietly pray these blessings as you go forward to receive Communion or as you kneel and meditate afterward. Whe you recieve the Body and Blood of Christ, remember that these channel Christ's life to you. This is the blessing of all blessings.

Blessing for Bread

Blessed are you
King of all creation
for this bread
which earth has given and human hands
    have made.
It will become for me the Bread of Life.

Blessing for Wine

Blessed are you
King of all creation
for this wine
fruit of the vine

work of human hands.
It will become my spiritual drink.

Lamb of God

Lamb of God
Defenseless Victor
Take from us our sin
Give to us the food of eternal life.

This Precious Nectar

This precious nectar is my delight.
From this cup flows warmth for my darkest night.
From you I drink in poise and power
Though I am broken, in a needy hour.
And cup-sharing with me, are rich and poor,
Folk of all kinds, all thirsty for more.

As I eat and drink, help me
to touch your utter, self-giving love.

Infant Blessing

Children need families; they need their mothers and fathers to make a commitment to them from the beginning. For most Catholics and many Protestants, this happens when the child is baptized. But not all parents wish to baptize their children soon after birth, and some people become adoptive parents or guardians of children who have already been baptized.

This service is for all parents who wish to give their child their loving commitment and God's blessing. It may take place anywhere — a church, a home, another building, a garden. Parents may ask a respected friend (a soul friend or anamchara) *to lead the service and to adapt it so that it fits their needs.*

Welcome

⁓

The leader says:

We welcome [*names of mother and father*] and join them in giving thanks for the gift of [*name of infant*] to be their *daughter/son,* and to be a new *brother/sister* for [*name(s) of any siblings or stepbrothers and stepsisters of the baby*].

We meet on this special day to celebrate the birth and naming of this child, to witness solemn undertakings on *her/his* behalf by *her/his* parents, and to ask God's blessing on this precious life.

Thanks

The leader may say:

God our Creator, in giving us this child you have shown us your love. We thank you from our hearts for the joy of this child, for the wonder of his life, for a safe delivery, and for the privilege of being parents.

Naming

The leader asks the parents:

You have brought your child to be welcomed into your circle of family and friends. What names have you chosen?

The parent(s) state the name(s). (The leader or a parent may explain the meaning of the names.)

Commitments

~

The leader asks the parent(s) the following questions:

Will you care for this child, feed and befriend *her/him*, listen to and play with *her/him*, keep *her/him* safe, and daily share your heart with *her/him*?

Parent(s):

I will.

Will you help your child, by your example and your teaching, to be honest, to be responsible, and to help others?

Parent(s):

I will.

Will you respect, encourage, and guide
her/him, and will you put *her/his* true needs
before your pleasure? Will you try to order
your lives so that your child will be surrounded
by love and goodness?

Parent(s):

I will.

For the sake of your child, will you remain
together and work at being good friends, even
in conflict? Will you say sorry when you are
wrong and forgive them when you are wronged?

Parent(s):

I will.

Do you dedicate your child to God?

Parent(s):

I do.

Do you dedicate yourselves to God, and do you promise, by God's help, to provide a Christian home for this child, to pray with your child, to teach your child about Christ, and to encourage your child to know and serve Christ?

Parent(s):

I do.

The leader asks the family friends the following questions:

Will you be a continuing friend to this child and be ready to help in times of special need?

Friends:

I will.

Will you pray for this child and give *her/him* opportunities to ask questions about your own journey through life?

Friends:

I will.

The leader asks any sisters, brothers, stepsisters, or stepbrothers:

Will you try to be kind and to share things with *her/him* and will you treat *her/his* parents and your parents with respect?

Sibling(s):

I will.

The leader asks the grandparent(s):

Will you do your best to give thoughtful support and encouragement as long as you live?

Grandparent(s):

I will.

The minister or soul friend says:

God bless you and help you to carry out these promises.

Words to Remember

The leader says:

When the people of Israel were first given guidance as to how to bring up their families, they were told:

> Israel, remember this! The LORD — and the LORD alone — is our God. Love the LORD your God with all your heart, with all your soul, and with all your strength. Never forget these commands that I am giving you today. Teach them to your children. Repeat them when you are at home and when you are away, when you are resting and when you are working. (Deuteronomy 6:4–7, *TEV*)

At this time, someone may sing a song, read a poem, or play a musical instrument.

**The leader reads from the Gospel according
to St. Mark:**

They brought children for [Jesus] to touch.
The disciples rebuked them, but when Jesus
saw this he was indignant, and said to them,
"Let the children come to me; do not try to
stop them; for the kingdom of God belongs to
such as these. I tell you, whoever does not
accept the kingdom of God like a child will
never enter it." And he put his arms round
them, laid his hands upon them, and blessed
them. (Mark 10:13 – 16, *NEB*)

**A card with the words of Deuteronomy 6:4 – 7
written on it may be given to the parents
to hang above the child's bedroom door. A
copy of a Gospel may also be presented to
the parents.**

The leader says:

We welcome [*name of infant*] as Jesus welcomed children. This book contains the good news of God's love. Read it, for it tells how you and your family may turn from evil, trust in Jesus Christ, and share in God's eternal purpose.

Gifts may be given, and prayers may be said.

The Circling Prayer and Blessing

A candle may be lit and given to the mother. Everyone stands in a circle around the baby and the mother.

The leader places a hand on the child's head and says:

Christ as light illumine and guide you. Christ as a shield overshadow you. Christ under you; Christ over you; Christ beside you; Christ ahead

of you; Christ within you. Christ in the heart
of a friend or stranger. Christ as your light, every
day of your life.

All say:

Circle *her/him*, Lord, keep harm without
Circle *her/him*, Lord, keep evil without
Circle *her/him*, Lord, keep strife without
Circle *her/him*, Lord, keep lies without
Circle *her/him*, Lord, keep hatred without.

**Any individuals may name something they
wish to be kept without.**

All say:

Circle *her/him*, Lord, keep peace within
Circle *her/him*, Lord, keep love within
Circle *her/him*, Lord, keep trust within
Circle *her/him*, Lord, keep truth within
Circle *her/him*, Lord, keep good within.

**Any individuals may name something they
wish to be kept within.**

The leader says one or all of the following prayers:

Father of love, accept the thanksgiving of these parents. May their spirits lift to you now in humble gratitude, always turn to you for help and strength. Give them wisdom, tenderness, and patience, to guide their child to know right from wrong.

Father, may [*names of mother and father*] be to the other a strength in need, a comfort in sorrow, a companion in joy. Knit their wills together in your will that they may live together in love, hope, and peace all their days.

May you respect one another;
May the goodness of friendship grow in you;
May the love that covers a multitude of sins be
    upon you.

God's peace be with you, whatever you do;
God's light to guide you wherever you go;
God's goodness to fill you and help you to grow.

Silence, singing, music, dancing, or feasting may follow.

*If these blessings do not fit with the wedding liturgy, pray
them right after the wedding or at the reception. They may
also be used for wedding anniversaries or for the renewal
of wedding vows.*

Wedding

Before the Start of
a Wedding Service

Open our eyes to your presence
Open our ears to your call
Open our hearts to your love.

After the Entrance of the Bride

Most powerful Spirit of God
Come down upon us and bless us
From heaven
Where the ordinary is made glorious

And glory seems but ordinary
Bathe us
With the brilliance
Of your light
Like dew.

The Word of the Lord

In Brittany a priest often leads the bridal couple in a walk around the person who will read from the Bible or Lectionary, which the reader holds up. This is a symbol of the journey through life that they are about to begin together. It is a way of saying, We do not know where our journey will lead, but wherever it leads, God's Word will be central to it.

Before the Vows

There may be a time of reflection focusing on the bride and groom to the accompaniment of soft bagpipe music. During this time anyone may write down prayers, sayings, or good wishes or draw pictures on pieces of paper provided. Here is an example of a prayer that can be written on a card and given out or read aloud:

May the Father take you
In his fragrant clasp of love
In every up and every down of your life.

The love and affection of God be with you
The love and affection of the angels be with you
The love and affection of the saints in heaven
    be with you
The love and affection of your friends on earth
    be with you
To guard you
To cherish you
To bring you to your eternal fulfillment.

Joining Hands after the Vows

May you be bound with unbreakable bonds
    of love to one another
May you be bound with unbreakable bonds
    of love to your God
May your love for each other reflect the love
    of your Maker, Savior, and Guide,
The Three of limitless love.

A Bridal Blessing after the Vows

May the Father take you in his fragrant clasp
    of love
May the Virgin Mary's Son guide you through
    the maze of life
May the generous Spirit release forgiving love
    within you,

Hour by hour, by day and by night, in joy and
    in failure
May all men and all women who are saints
    in heaven
Urge you on to complete your course.

Prayers for the Future

God's own presence with you stay
Jesus to shield you in the fray
Spirit to protect you from all ill
Trinity there guiding you still.

On sea or land, in ebb or flow,
God be with you wherever you go.
In flow or ebb, on land or sea
God's great might your protecting be.

Lord
let our memory
provide no shelter
for grievance against each other.

Lord
let our heart provide no harbor
for hatred of each other.

Lord
let our tongue
be no accomplice
in the judgment of each other.

Prayer for a New Household

May you be host to the great High King,
with all the company of heaven.
The sustenance of pure love be in your house,
the roots of repentance in your house.

Baskets of love be yours to give,
with cups of mercy for all the company.
May sweet Jesus, and all the company of
heaven, be there with you.

Circling

*Everyone, or invited persons, may form a circle around the
newly married couple and pray this blessing together:*

Circle them Lord
Keep love within, keep hate without
Circle them, Lord, keep faith within, keep
mistrust without.
Circle them, Lord, keep light within, keep
dark without.

Traditional Blessings

May the road rise to meet you.
May the wind be always at your back.
May the sun shine warm upon your face.
The rain fall soft upon your fields,
And until we meet again
May God hold you
In the hollow of his hand.

May the Sacred Three pour upon you mildly
and generously more and more forever.

The Reception

*Think carefully about the place as well as the building for
the reception. Celtic Christians have a strong sense of place.
I witnessed a Breton marriage celebration at the top of Mount
Dol. This combined in one place a sense of prayer (there was
a chapel), a place for eating (there was a restaurant and picnic
tables), a place for dancing, and a beautiful view — all of which
could be captured well on video or in photographs.*

3
Daily and Seasonal

Daily Rituals

Washing

I wash my face in the sun
In the nine rays of the sun
As Mary washed her Son
In the rich fermented milk.

Love be in my countenance,
Benevolence in my mind,
Dew of honey in my tongue
My breath as the incense.

From the Carmina Gadelica

Mealtime Blessings

May this food restore our strength,
give new energy to tired limbs, new thoughts to
    weary minds.
May this drink restore our souls,
give new vision to dry spirits, new warmth to
    cold hearts.
And once refreshed,
may we give new pleasure to you, who gives
    us all.

May the blessing of the five loaves and the
    two fishes
which God shared out among the five thousand,
    be ours.
May the King who did the sharing bless
    our sharing.

Bless, O Lord, this food we are about to eat; and
    we pray to you,
O God, that it may be good for our body and soul;
and if there be any poor creature hungry or
    thirsty walking along the road,
send them into us that we can share the food
    with them,
just as you share your gifts with all of us.

Bless us, O God, bless our food and our drink.
Since it is you who bought us at such great price,
save us from all evil.

Give us, O God of the nourishing meal,
Well-being to the body, the frame of the soul.
Give us, O God of the honey-sweet milk,
The sap and the savior of the fragrant farms.

Some have meat and cannot eat;
Some cannot eat that want it:
But we have meat and we can eat
Sae let the Lord be thankit!

Robert Burns, adapted

God in our waking, God in our speaking;
God in our cooking, God in our eating;
God in our laughing, God in our digesting;
God in our working, God in our resting.

May this food so fresh and fragrant
Call forth reverence for you.
As you give this strength to our perishable limbs,
So give us grace for our eternal lives.

Thanks to you for the abundance of food,
For the bounty of creation,
For all that is good.

In a world where so many are hungry,
May we eat this food with humble hearts;
In a world where so many are lonely,
May we share this friendship with joyful hearts.

Bless you, King of the universe,
For this sign of your tender care.
Bless you, King of this eating room
For this sign that you are here.
Bless you, Creator of all we eat;
Bless you, Savior — you with us meet;
Bless you, Spirit who makes this sweet.

You who put beam in moon and sun,
You who put food in ear and herd,
You who put fish in stream and sea,
Put a grateful heart in me.

Blessed are you, High King of the universe,
It is of your goodness we have this food to eat
   and this wine to drink,
Blessed be you forever!

Bless, O Lord, this food which we are about to
   eat for our bodily welfare.
May we be strengthened thereby to do your
   holy will.

Glory, praise and thanks to you, O God, for this
   food and our good health.
We also thank you for all the food and health for
   which we have not thanked you.

A thousand thanks to you, O God, who has
   given us this food for the body.
Grant us we ask you, who are so generous,
   eternal life.

After Food

A thousand thanks to you, O King of the
    universe;
a thousand thanks to you, O Lord of grace,
for what you have given us since our birth,
and for what you will give us until the day of
    our death.
Thanks be to you, O God, praise be to you,
    O God,
Reverence be to you, O God, for all you have
    given me.
As you have given physical life to earn me my
    worldly food,
So grant me eternal life to show forth your glory.

Sleep

Sleep in peace
Sleep soundly
Sleep in love.
Weaver of dreams
Weave well in you as you sleep.

I lie down this night
Near the King of Life
Near Christ of the destitute
Near the Holy Spirit.
I lie down this night
With the angels
From the crown of my head
To the soles of my feet;
From the crown of my head
To the soles of my feet.

From the Carmina Gadelica

Day and Night

Morning

Encircle my soul
In morning stillness
Scatter the shadows of fear

Be at my side in midday bustle
Weave through the knotwork of time

Talk to my heart
In teatime chatter
Speak through the discords of life

Lighten the load
Of incoming darkness
Glow like a star at midnight.

Jane M. Mackichan

Rising

I arise today
In the strength of the mighty Creator
In the strength of the rising Savior
In the strength of the life-giving Spirit
In the strength of the mighty Three
Whose love is One.

I arise today
In the strength of the angels and archangels
In the strength of the prophets and apostles
In the strength of the martyrs and saints

I arise today
In the strength of heaven and earth
In the strength of sun and moon
In the strength of fire and wind

I arise today
In the strength of Christ's birth and baptism
In the strength of Christ's death and rising
In the strength of Christ's judgment to come.

Midday

We draw aside at the heart of the day
To seek your face and watch and pray
Refresh us, O Lord, and close to us stay
When we leave here and go our way.

As with manna you fed your fleeing folk
Like much-needed rain on the parched,
    dry ground
Refresh us now as your name we invoke
Come like dew, in power, on us.

Andrew Dick, from a song by the band Kentigern

Evening

Tonight, God of rest
As I lay down in bed
I rest:

my hopes	my fears
my longings	my thankfulness
my being	my non-being
my anxieties	my faith
my decisions	my indecisions
my work	my contemplation

that which is complete
that which is incomplete

my seeing	my darkness
my hearing	my deafness
my feeling	my hardness
my openness	my closedness
my past	my future

myself, in God, the community of the Three in me.

Carole Parker, adapted

Night

May we rest this night in the stillness
    of your being.

O Radiant Dawn, splendor of eternal light,
come and shine on us
that we may sleep in the warmth of your radiance.

O Emmanuel, God with us, we will lie down
    with you and you will lie down with us.

And the dawn shall come and so will
    your appearing
and we shall know as we are known
And in pleasure you will receive us.

Call forth this night bearers of your presence.
Call forth this night believers in your truth.

Seasonal

Holidays

Blessing of sun be yours
Blessing of earth be yours
Blessing of rock be yours
Blessing of sky be yours
Blessing of wind be yours
Blessing of water be yours
Blessing of fun be yours
Blessing of stillness be yours
Blessing of discovery be yours
Blessing of rest be yours
Blessing of meeting be yours
Blessing of thought be yours
Blessing of change be yours
Blessing of homecoming be yours.

New Year

God bless me to this year
Never vouchsafed to me before.
It is to bless your own presence
that you have given me this moment, O Lord.

Bless to me my eye
And everything it shall see
Bless to me my neighbor
May my neighbor be a blessing to me.

Bless to me my household
and all my dear ones
Bless to me my work and all that belongs
   to your provision.

Give to me a clean heart
That I may not need to hide from you
One moment of this new year.

Easter

My Christ rise in glory
Scattering the darkness before your path.

The Sun of suns,
the eye of the great God.
The eye of the King of Hosts,
is rising upon us,
gently and generously.
Welcome, glorious Son,
dawn of a new day.
Glory to you, Son of the Most High,
human face of God,
laboring with us, spending your life for us,
cross-bound to set us free.

Living One,
sword bright,
first and last,
banish all fear
from our hearts and minds.
Forgive us our sin.
On each of our dyings
shed your lovely light.
Bright face of God,
warmed by your glory,
may we run with joy to tell others
as you go ahead of us
into the world.

Kate McIlhagga

Halloween

God of time
God of dark
God of earth
God of heaven,
You are
Stronger than the elements,
Stronger than the shadows,
Stronger than the fears,
Stronger than human wills,
Stronger than the spirits,
Stronger than magic spells.

Your presence be our shield
The love of God to enfold us;
The peace of God to still us;
The spirit of God to fill us;
The saints of God to inspire us;
The angels of God to guard us
This night, this winter, forever.

Christmas

Child of Glory
Child of Mary
Born in the stable
The King of all
You came to our wasteland
In our place suffered
Draw near to us who to you call.

Bless to us this day of joy
Open to us heaven's generous gates
Strengthen our hope
Revive our tired souls
'Til we sing the joys of your glory
With all the angels of heaven.

Christmas Tree

Bless, O Lord, this Christmas Tree,
all that goes on to it
and all that goes on around it.

May the decorations remind us to buy things in
a spirit of joy, thoughtfulness, and generosity.

May the needles that fall to the ground make us
mindful of the needs of the poor and
homeless people the world over.

May the branches that point upwards lead us to
wonder and worship the Creator who came
from heaven to earth as a little child.

All Living Things

Tree of Life

O, King of the Tree of Life,
The blossoms on the branches are your people,
The singing birds are your angels,
The whispering breeze is your Spirit.

O, King of the Tree of Life,
May the blossoms bring forth the sweetest fruit,
May the birds sing out the highest praise,
May your Spirit cover all with his gentle breath.

From the Carmina Gadelica

Harvest

*Here is a way of celebrating harvest with a silent blessing: Build
a Celtic-shaped cross (the cross with a circle around it) on
the floor, using flowers, stones, fruit, greenery, etc. Form a circle*

around this. Take seven steps slowly to the right, then turn to
the center, bend, pick up a harvest item, slowly offer this to God
for a count of ten, and replace it. Repeat. This becomes a form
of corporate meditative prayer for harvest.

May God
who clothes the flowers
and feeds the birds of the sky,
who leads the lambs to pasture
and the deer to water,
who multiplied loaves and fishes
and changed water into wine
lead us
feed us
multiply us
and change us
until we reflect
the glory of our Creator
through all eternity.

Plants

There is no plant in the ground
But is full of your virtue
O King of the virtues.
May these plants bring your blessing to us.

There is no life in the earth
But proclaims your goodness.
O King of goodness
May these plants bring your goodness to us.

As I look at their leaves turned face to the sun
May I look towards you until this day is done.
As I admire the bright flowers
Giving glory to you
May I bring you pleasure in the things that I do.
As I look at the fruit tasty and sweet
May I taste of you to the people I meet.

Craig Roberts

Gardens

∿

It is good to bless a new garden, a relandscaped garden, or even a new season for a garden.

There is no plant in the ground
That does not tell of your beauty, Lord.
May this garden speak to us of the fragrance of
 your love.
May the fruits of the earth speak to us of
 your mercy.

Bless the moon that is above us;
The earth that is beneath us;
The hard work to be done here

The seedlings that shall grow here;
The neighbors we shall greet here;
And all who overlook here.

Pets

Many people have repeated the blessing St. Brigid of Ireland used to place upon her calves, goats, horses, and lambs. The following blessings for pets reflect this:

Each day and each night
In cold and heat
In light and dark
Keep them from falling
Keep them from road accidents
Keep them from thieves
Keep them from poisons
Keep them content
O sweet Maker of all.

[*Name of pet*],
the eye of God be on you
to bless you
to look after you
to give you pleasure
and to make you a pleasure.

The Creation

Dear planet
The Light of all light shine on you
The Power of all power energize you
The Love of all love win you.

May you become aware
that the Eternal Three
caress without ceasing
all forms, all realities
with graces, energies
and creative manifestations.

May you be unhindered by human egotism.

May consciousness of the One in Three dawn
 upon you.
May cooperation with the Three develop
 upon you.
May you move forward into your divine destiny.

4

Journey through Life

Human life is so precious that it calls out to be taken seriously.
Each human life is a journey, and on this journey there are
some important turning points. These need to be properly marked
so that we don't become confused or lost. We all need landmarks
in order to make sense of our lives. In this section, a blessing
is provided for significant turning points on our journey. These
should help to transform each turning point into a landmark.

Ancient Celtic people focused on four stars that are the fourfold
cloaks worn upon the circuit of life. The following is a Christian
prayer that reflects this understanding:

Lord of the elements, give us a good journey
    through life
Lord of the Star of the East, give us a kindly birth
Lord of the Star of the South, give us a great love
Lord of the Star of the West, give us a quiet age
Lord of the Star of the North, give us a blest death.

Special Days

Birth

∾

*I know a woman who is a scientist and was an atheist —
until the birth of her first baby, which flooded her with a
sense of wonder at the miracle of a new life. Most of us
need to express this sense of wonder, but we do not always
have the words to do so.*

*These blessings are inspired by prayers used in the Scottish
Highlands and Islands. These people had a conviction
that to look into the face of a newborn child is to see a
reflection of God. The blessings may be said by a midwife,
relative, or friend on the day of birth or soon after.
If others are present, they can say the "Amen," which
means "Yes!"*

The speaker says to a child:

The lovely likeness of the Lord in your face.

Three drops of warm water are poured on the baby's forehead, one during each of the first three sentences.

A little drop of your Creator
On your forehead, precious one.

All:

Amen.

A little drop of your Savior
On your forehead, precious one.
All:
Amen.

A little drop of your Savior
On your forehead, precious one.
All:
Amen.

A little drop of your Guardian Spirit
On your forehead, precious one.
All:
Amen.

A little drop of the Three
to shield you from harm
To fill you with their virtue.
All:
Amen.

Birthdays

~&

This blessing may be written out and given to someone
on their birthday. But do not neglect your own birthday. Why
not light a candle and slowly, with time for reflection, say
this blessing for yourself?

Joy of birth be yours today
Joy of memory be yours today
Joy of life be yours today
Joy of goodness be yours today
Joy of creation be yours today
Joy of friendship be yours today
Joy of giving be yours today
Joy of maturing be yours today
Joy of being known be yours today
Joy of self-knowing be yours today
Joy of Shepherd Father be yours today
Joy of Mary's Son be yours today
Joy of Friendly Spirit be yours today
Joy of eternal life be yours today
And forever.

Anniversaries

The joy of that day be in your face
The joy that made you grow in grace
The joy of memory be yours today
The joy of growth along the way
May you be joy to all who meet you
God's angels be always there to greet you
The circle of Christ around your neck
That day in heaven may you ne'er forget.
On this your anniversary
God give you the best of memories
Christ give you pardon for failings
Spirit give you the fruits of friendship.

Dark Times

Loss

All of us experience loss in one way or another, for it can come in many forms. We may suffer, for example, the loss of children, health, home, job, limb, or spouse.

Bruised?
The blessing of acceptance be yours.

Bitter?
The blessing of forgiveness be yours.

Angry?
The blessing of gentleness be yours.

Suicidal?
The blessing of trust be yours.

Broken?
The blessing of immortality be yours.

A Lonely Soul

In the stillness
See the wonder of God's art
In the silence
Feel Christ's presence
In the sunlight
Watch the Holy Spirit dance
In the darkness
Find faith's essence.

Jane M. Machickan

Despair

⤶

*Despair can be caused by crushing disappointments. Often,
however, it is caused by painful experiences that lie deeply buried
under the surface of our everyday consciousness. Sometimes,
sanity-destroying flashbacks bring these to mind. If you get such
a flashback, focus on an image of Christ being crucified, and
say a blessing on yourself in this pit of despair.*

Christ of the agony
Christ of the bleeding
Christ racked and stretched out on the Tree
I place upon you my own agony
I place upon you my bleeding heart
I place upon you my despair.

Take it
Break it
Remake it.
Your Tree of death became the Tree of Life;
Give your blessing of life to me.

Victim of Crime

Into your loss
Come
O Being of Gift
O Being of Peace
O Being of Life eternal.

Into your threat
Come
O Being of Strength
O Being of Peace
O Being of Life eternal.

Into your despair
Come
O Being of Hope
O Being of Peace
O Being of Life eternal

Into your devastation
Come
O Being of Love
O Being of Peace
O Being of Life eternal.

Battered People

Gentle Father
Bless these battered children.
Take the hurt out of their lives.
May your gentle spirit flow
through all those who care for them.

Tender Savior
Bless these battered wives
Take the fear out of their lives.
May your tender spirit flow
through all those who care for them.

Caressing Spirit
Bless these elderly who feel battered
by their children's rejection.
Take resentment out of their lives.
May your caressing spirit flow
through all those who care for them.

Infertility

Call forth life within us.

Father of life
Bless the swarming sperm
that teems with life so manifold.
Spirit of life
Bless the welcoming egg
that patiently waits to conceive.
Savior of Life
Change the barren water of this womb
into a winelike ferment of life.

Call forth life within us.

Bless to us, O God, the anguish that is ours.
Change the stagnant void in our hearts
into a life-giving stream
That we may become pregnant with fresh
    creativity
Love pouring forth abundantly from us
Mothering and fathering an orphaned world
Bringing to flower the seed you have planted
    in us
Faith and joy outpouring.

Divorce

Grant me
acceptance of pain without bitterness
grieving for loss without blame
forgiveness for frailty without remorse
renewal of trust without fear.

Sadness and sin behind us be
Farewell to marriage, but friends let us be.
Bless our children in their hurts
Bless us as parents with our warts.

Job Loss

Bless to me, O God,
this loss, that I may grow through grieving
this worry, that I may learn through trusting
this space, that I may develop through creating
this grim bureaucrat, that I may become
    gracious through bearing.

God bless to you this loss
that you may know the eternal boss.
God bless you in being poor
that Providence will open its door.
God bless to you this "grave"
that you may know that Christ can save.

Take Me under Your Protection

Take me under your protection O beloved
    angel of God, just as the Lord of grace
    so ordained. Accompany me at all times
    and protect me from worry and danger.

I ask for the Light of Light, the vision
    of the Trinity,
And the grace of patience in the face
    of injustice.

Life is but a passing shadow,
our stay here is but for a time.
But we will have good weather after the
    final raindrop.

O God, all powerful, you are my strength.
O Lord of all the world, my life is yours.
Whatever be your will, may it be done.

O Lord, give me your grace and your love,
    and I will be safe forevermore.

Death

Of an Enemy

This soul did little good to me, O Lord,
But this soul was yours.

So to this soul I say:
I bless the day you were born
I bless your growing up
I bless you, even in your dark deeds
And I bless you, soul, at your end.

Travel to the God who transforms
Travel to the Arms so wide
Travel to the Spirit all generous.

Of an Unborn Child

The mother says:

Dear God, the child (or children) who was lost through abortion is mine and yours.

Dear God, I am sorry that I have forgotten and ignored them. I ask their forgiveness and yours. It helps to know that no child is lost to you.

First, I wish to say I am especially sorry that the life of my [*first, second, etc.*] child was taken through abortion. I am grateful, Lord, that you know all the pressures, the difficulties, and the problems that caused me to make that decision. Whatever my reasons, Lord, I am truly sorry for the taking of this life. I ask forgiveness from you and from the child who has died. I acknowledge before you that this was truly a child and was truly my own. I place this child into your tender care; I assure *her/him* of my love.

A minister or soul friend says:

We release [*name of aborted child*] into your hands. May your blessing and your peace be upon *her/him*. Bring *her/him* to wholeness in your eternal kingdom.

Parents say:

Now, dear Jesus, I wish to name before you the one who was born on [*date*]. In faith I name *her/him*. I ask you to heal *her/him* of any shock or hurt *s/he* has carried as a result of the way *s/he* died.

A minister or soul friend says:

Lord Jesus, in your name we break the power of the past to have a hold over [*name of parent*]. May the cross of Christ come between you and your past. The love of Jesus fill you, a lamb of his choosing, that you may rest in his arms and walk free into the fruitful paths he has for you.

A cross, flower, plant, or plaque may be put in a place of remembrance.

Three drops of water may be poured on that spot, using this prayer for a baby:

A little drop of your Creator, precious one.
A little drop of your Savior, precious one.
A little drop of your Guardian Spirit,
    precious one.
To bless you with virtue and sweetness,
To keep you in eternal life.

All:

Amen.

There may be singing or words of praise and encouragement. If desired, there may be the laying on of hands in silent or spoken prayer:

May the tender and gracious God pour out love
    upon you
May you walk free and walk tall.
May the Creator's power protect you

The Savior's care enfold you
The Spirit's life renew you.
May you walk in the fragrant clasp
of the Three of limitless love
now and forever.

*These prayers are suitable for occasions when the life in me
seems to be ebbing or when I want to prepare myself, while in
full strength, for my final journey from this life.*

At Journey's End

As you were there
Before my life's beginning
Be there again
At my journey's end.

As you were there
At my soul's shaping
Father, be there too,
At my soul's close.

Savior and Friend, how wonderful art Thou,
My companion upon the changeful way,
The comforter of its weariness,
My guide to the Eternal Town,
The welcome at its gate.

Hebridean altars

I am going home with you, to your home,
   to your home;
I am going home with you, to your home
   of mercy.
I am going home with you, to your home,
   to your home;
I am going home with you, to the Fount of all
   the blessings.

Adapted from the Carmina Gadelica

Alone

Alone with none but you, my God,
I journey on my way.
What need I fear, when you are near,
O King of night and day?
More safe am I within your hand
Than if a host did round me stand.

My life I yield to your command,
And bow to your control;
In peaceful calm, for from your arm
No power can snatch my soul.
Could earthly foes ever appall
A soul that heeds the heavenly call!

Attributed to St. Columba

Drawing My Soul

O great God of heaven, draw my soul to you;
Give to me sincere repentance.
O Healer of my soul, bestow on me forgiveness;
Give to me joy and gladness.
O great God of life, breathe through me your life,
Give to me strong Spirit of powers.
O gracious God of angels, bathe me in your light;
Give to me the loving spirit of the Lamb.

Echoes a prayer in the Carmina Gadelica

Protecting Body and Soul

My good angel, messenger of God,
Protect my body and my soul;
Protect me from the evil spirit
And above all else from sin.
I pray you, saints, men and women,
I pray you, Jesus,
To protect me and obtain for me
A good and happy death.

Britanny

*As in the Highlands and Islands, blessings over a dying person
may be said by an* anamchara *(soul friend) or by a priest,
another minister, or a relative, with others. These death blessings
are sometimes known as "soul leading" or "soul peace." The soul
peace should be said slowly (unless it is sung, as in the isles),
with all present joining the dying person in asking the Three
Persons of the Trinity and the saints in heaven to receive the
departing soul. During the prayer, the soul friend, minister, or
relative makes the sign of the cross on the forehead of the dying
person. (In the isles, it is made over the lips with the thumb.)*

*Even with people who have little religious background,
a well-known Bible passage, psalm, or hymn (e.g., "Abide with
Me") may be read along with one or more of the prayers that
follow. A cross may be held in front of them.*

Sorrow

Sleep, sleep, and away with sorrow,
Sleep in the arms of Jesus.
Sleep in the breast of virgin Mother,
Sleep in the calm of all calm,
Sleep in the love of all loves.
Sleep in the Lord of life eternal.

Adapted from the Carmina Gadelica

Beloved Soul

May kindly Michael, Chief of the holy angels,
Take charge of your beloved soul,
And tenderly bring it home
To the Three of limitless love,
Creator, Savior, Life-giver.

Adapted from the Carmina Gadelica

The Circling Prayer

This may be used as a prayer for oneself using "me" and "my."

The Holy Three encircle you
The Saving Three release you
The Eternal Three keep you
May the Loving Three caress you and work in you,
In your loved one,
In those you have lost,
In your dark,
In your day,
In your pain,
In your seeing,
In your journey,
In eternity.

God Be with You

God be with you today and forever
Jesus be in you to pardon and tether
Spirit be on you and leave you never.

In the name of the all-powerful Father,
In the name of the all-loving Son,
In the name of the all-pervading Spirit,
I command all spirits of fear to leave you,
I break the power of unforgiven sin in you,
I set you free from dependence upon human ties
That you may be as free as the wind,
As soft as a sheep's wool,
As straight as an arrow,
And that you may journey into the heart of God.

Growing Up

Falling in Love
‿❧

*The resurgence of interest in the legends of the Celtic King
Arthur reflects a deep longing to discover a way of loving
that has true romance, chivalry, and fidelity. Despite
the widespread cheapening of sex, it seems something
deep in the human heart does not want it to be like that.
The Arthurian myths can help young people visualize
an alternative way of loving. But if this is to become a
reality, the alternative way needs to be marked at the
time when attraction to the opposite sex first awakens.*

*This blessing can be written out and given to sons,
daughters, or friends at the time when they reveal their
first romantic feelings.*

Bless this thing that sparks like lightning
That burns like fire
That radiates like the inside of the first
    moment of the cosmos
In this awakening love may there always be
courtesy and respect
trust and courage
tenderness and truth.

Take from it all that destroys and is willful
Give to it all that lasts and is selfless
That the one may wither and the other may
　　grow strong
And shine forever.
God bless this one whom I feel such love for.
May I never cheapen this love
May I never use the other just to gratify
　　my appetites
May I always be there for the other
May this love be like a flower that slowly opens
　　up to reveal its full beauty
May I offer my beloved a heart of valor,
　　restraint, and service.

Leaving Home

May God look after you wherever you go
May the everlasting Father take you in his
    generous clasp
May Christ lead you to your true destination
May the Spirit bathe you in heavenly light.

May the saints and the angels stretch out their
    arms for you
When you are tempted
When you go through rough places
When you return home.

The peace of the Son of peace be with you
And your children's children
Each day and each night
Of your life in this world.

Parties and Nights Out

Circle us, Lord
Keep these graces within:
The grace of form
The grace of beauty
The grace of movement
The grace of eating
The grace of conversation
The grace of laughter
The grace of listening
The grace of restraint
The grace of self-forgetfulness.

Circle us, Lord
Keep these evils without:
The evil of fear
The evil of boasting
The evil of pretense
The evil of excess
The evil of abuse
The evil of addiction.

Manhood: A Boy's First Steps

~&

*In most societies, when a boy reaches puberty, he is separated
from his mother, and his father or his father's peers take him off
to face the world outside of the home, to learn to tackle things,
to work, to stand on his own feet.*

*In our society, too, it is possible to mark this stage for a boy or
a girl. A father or a leader in a local organization or church
might take the youngster away for an activity weekend. Before
the boy leaves, his parents might place their hands on his
shoulders or head and give a blessing such as the following:*

God help you to:
run straight
speak what is true
ask questions
overcome fear
learn self-control
bear failure
stand alone
care for your body
guard your soul
honor women

respect men
explore the world
give your best
open your heart to all people
close your heart to all pretense
know yourself
reverence the Creator
walk with the Savior
flow with the Spirit
enter into your eternal destiny.

Womanhood: A Girl's First Period

This is a blessing of the God of life
The blessing of mild mother Mary
From whose breasts our Lord suckled milk.

May God give you strength in every such time
May Christ give you love in every such time
May Spirit give you peace in every such time.

Lord, place these nine choice graces
in the upturned face
of this day's wakened lass:
the grace of deportment
the grace of voice
the grace of provision
the grace of goodness
the grace of wisdom
the grace of caring
the grace of femininity
the grace of a lovely personality
the grace of godly speech.

Aging

Midlife Crisis

Life passes by?
Blessing of letting go be yours.

Fear of losing out?
Blessing of lowly spirit be yours.

Driven by false ambition?
Blessing of having nothing be yours.

Flight from chaos within?
Blessing of true being be yours.

Anger at failing before others?
Blessing of eternal reward be yours.

Weary of timeworn patterns?
Blessing of dawn be yours.

Losing faith in your peers?
Blessing of angels be yours.

Disillusioned even with life?
Blessing of resurrection be yours.

Middle Age

*I once came across a prayer for middle age written by a
Carmelite friar. It inspired the following blessing for someone
who is beginning to grow old.*

God keep you from
having to say something on every occasion,
having to sort out everyone else's affairs,
reciting endless details.
God give you wings to get to the point.

God seal your lips on your aches and pains.

God keep you reasonably sweet,
for a sour old person is one of the crowning
    works of the devil.

God help you to endure with patience others'
    tales of woe.

God give you
an ability to see good things in unexpected places,
talents in unexpected people,
and the grace to tell them so.

God
keep you from evil within,
shield you from evil without,
bless you with virtue and sweetness,
aid you in times of trial.

God
give you pluck and valor,
bring you good health and good speech,
save you for good and for God,
the One and the Three who is love.

Retirement

Wisdom of years be yours
Joy of friendships be yours
Wealth of memories be yours
Fruit of endeavor be yours
Hope of heaven be yours
Peace of God be yours.

Old Age

This blessing reflects Psalm 92:4.

May you be evergreen and full of sap
and bear fruit each day of your life.

*Celtic people were impressed by the fact that three trees — holly,
mistletoe, and yew — kept their leaves green throughout the
year. They thought that these trees symbolized certain things
in human lives that were meant to remain evergreen, even
if other parts of life fell away in old age. This blessing reflects
that insight:*

As holly, mistletoe, and yew
keep their leaves green throughout the year
so may these three things
be kept evergreen in you —
respect, restraint, and reverence for life.

Welcoming Arms

The welcome of the Father's arms be yours
The welcome of the Savior's heart be yours
The welcome of the Spirit's call be yours.

Deep peace of this earth to you
Deep peace of this sky to you
Deep peace of this place to you.

The kindly eye of the Three be upon you
To aid you and guard you
To cherish and enrich you.

May God take you in the clasp of his own
    two hands.

Finally

May everything in you be blessed;
and may you bless every one
and every thing.

May you be bathed in the blessings
that the Great Blesser
delights to shower upon you.

May you be saved from the sourness
that corrodes the person
who neglects to bless.

Bring forth buds of hope
Bring fruitfulness to this stagnant earth
May flowers and beauty bloom on it
May friendships grow on it
May songs burst forth
And dancing, loving, creating after stagnant,
   barren years.

The blessing of God and the Lord be yours,
The blessing of the perfect Spirit be yours,
The blessing of the Three be pouring on you
mildly and generously, more and more
and forever.

Acknowledgments and Sources

Many of the prayers in this book echo blessings in the *Carmina Gadelica* collected and translated into English by Alexander Carmichael. Published by Floris Books, Edinburgh, 1992.

Many of the mealtime blessings echo those in *Traditional Irish Prayers* collected and translated into English by Paidrecha Ilghneitheacha and published by Mount Melleray Abbey, Waterford, Ireland.

Some of the prayers for the sick and for baptism were previously published as separate sheets by the Community of Aidan and Hilda.

The prayers "Bless the car . . ." on p. 45 and "Tonight, God of rest . . ." on p. 101 are copyright Carole Parker, first published in *The Aidan Way*, the magazine of the Community of Aidan and Hilda, c/o Lindisfarne Retreat, Holy Island, Berwick-upon-Tweed TD15 2SD England.

I am indebted to Keith Hitchman for some suggestions for the wedding blessings.

The wedding prayer "Lord, let our memory provide no shelter" is from *Celtic Night Prayer — Cuthbert — into a desert place* published by HarperCollins, © 1996 The Northumbria Community Trust and used with permission.

The Easter blessing "Glory to you" is copyright Kate McIlhagga and is from *Encompassing Presence*, the Prayer Handbook for 1993 published by the United Reformed Church in the U.K.

I would also like to thank the following for the use of their prayers:

Andrew Dick for his adaptation of my prayer in the song by Kentigern "We draw aside at the heart of the day . . ." on p. 100; Jane M. Mackichan for her prayer "In the stillness . . ." on p. 98; Craig Roberts for his prayer "As I look at their leaves . . ." on p. 112; USA Festival of Names Church for the prayer "In blessing our foreheads . . ." on pp. 28 – 29; Esther de Waal for her prayer "I program my computer . . ." on p. 27.